In Memory of

Alice C. Panitz

TOULOUSE-LAUTREC

Lautrec

BY EDOUARD JULIEN

CROWN PUBLISHERS INC. ▪ NEW YORK

1959

Title page: SELF PORTRAIT OF TOULOUSE-LAUTREC. 1880.
Museum Toulouse-Lautrec, Albi.

Translated by:
HELEN C. SLONIM

PRINTED IN ITALY.

On the Promenade des Anglais. 1879. Watercolour. Private Collection.

Looking back upon my youth, I can still picture quite vividly the deformed shape of Henri de Toulouse-Lautrec, as I used to see it in the streets of Albi when the painter came over for the holidays to rest and visit his family in the house where he had been born.

Count Alphonse, the artist's father, was himself an especially original figure in Albi. One would frequently meet him in town; he would be in eccentric array, holding his favorite hawk on his closed fist; for this aristocrat was a fervent hunter and one of the last devotees of hawking.

His freakish outbursts would delight us children, especially when he invited us to participate. I can still picture him as he came one day to meet us when we were leaving the *Lycée*, carrying on his broad shoulders a load of graceful and frail Japanese kites which he suggested we try flying around the Cathedral Sainte-Cécile in order to get them as high as the steeple.

We were always sure to find the Count around the booths when there was a fair going on; or near the circus or the menageries. Fascinated by animals he would hastily sketch their movements which he later interpreted in clay, for he tried modelling when he felt like it.

He associated with all the artists from the circus and would soon become friendly with them, and went so far as to advise them.

One evening he even was the unexpected star of the show given by the Bureau circus in our town. The director's very young daughter was taking her first steps in equestrian acrobatics, safely secured by a rope which her father held; he was ready to jump to her rescue in case

Child's Head: Séverino Rossi. 1883. Drawing. Museum Toulouse-Lautrec, Albi.

of faltering. As soon as the gracious rider had gone back to the wings, under hearty applause, the crowd was taken aback to see Count Alphonse make his entrance with a young cousin of his. The latter impersonated the little girl on the horse, while the Count, with a dead-pan face took over the part of father Bureau. The renewed and praiseworthy efforts of the two partners only resulted in a spectacular failure to the greatest delight of both the public and the circus personnel.

Indifferent to criticism, the Count was a perfect gentleman whose life consisted in satisfying his fantasies and his whims, keeping an unperturbed dignity under any circumstances. However, his eccentricities have been wantonly multiplied and many of them are sheer legend.

If one goes back through the centuries, the ancestral filiation reveals the origin of an heredity from which neither Count Alphonse nor his son Henri escaped.

The painter's paternal ancestries are the famous hereditary counts of Toulouse, which since Charlemagne had held the vast country of Albigeois; also the powerful viscounts of Lautrec whose fiefs covered the counties of Quercy, Albi, Béziers, Nîmes and part of the Provence. These gallant and turbulent warriors, which adversity never deterred, took part in all the crusades — including the one against Catharism — in the religious and civil wars, and in the Spanish wars. From Henri IV on, royalty could not have had more faithful champions. The Toulouse-Lautrecs always took up a military career and Count Alphonse followed this tradition.

The painter's mother's family, the Tapiés, originated from Azille in the Minervois where they had been residing since the XIIIth century. Several consuls were numbered among the family members. During the XVIth century they settled in Narbonne, and their descendants remained in the King's service as magistrates, canons, and general treasurers, becoming landowners, clever at developing their estates and their vines. They were generally held in high esteem. Following the southern custom the name of their estate, Céleyran, was added to their own.

Since the beginning of the XIXth century, the Tapié de Céleyran and the Toulouse-Lautrec had united through numerous alliances and intermarriages.

The marriage of Adèle Tapié de Céleyran with Count Alphonse de Toulouse-Lautrec, her first cousin, followed the tradition. The idea was to unite and preserve the wealthy inheritance of both families.

A cloudless future seemed to be in store for this splendid couple full of health and prospects.

Just before getting married, the handsome Lancer officer resigned his military duties, under the pretense of looking after his expanded estate; it was really in order to satisfy his craving for independence.

The couple was living at the Chateau du Bosc, in Aveyron, when the Countess felt with delight the first indications of maternity. To await the birth of the son she was hoping for, she preferred settling in the town of Albi, in the house belonging to her aunts, Mesdemoiselles Imbert du Bosc. This house, later acquired by inheritance, was to become the main dwelling of the Toulouse-Lautrec family, known as the Hotel du Bosc.

It was there that Henri-Marie de Toulouse-Lautrec-Monfa was born during the night of December 24th, 1864 while a storm was raging over the town. Later on the Countess considered the breaking out of the storm as an ill-omen. The baby was handsome and promised to become worthy of his ancestors.

The Countess was overwhelmed by an infinite maternal love which was to burst out intensely during the cruel period which later brought accidents, illness and dejection, which she desperately fought.

Henri grew, but never became a strong child. Count Alphonse imposed a new dwelling on his family: Loury-aux-Bois in the forest of Orléans, where he could hunt big game.

Deserted, betrayed and scoffed, the Countess returned to Albi, leaving in the earth of Orléans her second son Richard who had lived less than a year.

She was an attentive mother and a cultured woman, and decided to bring up Henri alone. She carefully chose the tutors who were to help in this task. In the old family house, Henri was to find a more favorable atmosphere for his education.

But the Count, imposing his will once more, decided that the family would go and live in Paris.

Henri who is eight years old becomes a pupil in the eighth preparatory grade of the Lycée Fontanes (now Lycée Condorcet). His mind is quick. Although far from being studious, he is a good pupil, and succeeds, even getting the excellence prize.

His best friends are Louis Pascal, his cousin, and Maurice Joyant (1864-1931) whose solid friendship — despite a break of several years — will persist until death. He will be Henri's best biographer and strongest champion.

His parents' numerous trips handicap the boy's work. The family returns once more to Albi where Henri will share a first class education with his many cousins.

His taste for drawing, which started when he was very young, becomes an imperious necessity. The margins of his exercise and other books are copiously illustrated with witty and accurate sketches, mostly of horses. In the family circle everybody has a look at his Zig-zag book, an illustrated story of a stay in Nice with his mother, « dedicated to his cousin Madeleine Tapié de Céleyran, with the commendable aim of diverting her a little from Mademoiselle de Vergnettes' lessons. »

The Countess is enthusiastic about her son's talent; she encourages him in his already promising attempts; but she is incessantly worried about Henri's health which demands numerous stays in the country at the Chateau du Bosc at Céleyran, where the Countess was born. Then Amélie-les-Bains and Nice are prescribed. Alas, none of these changes bring about the expected improvement.

However, Henri is always gay, lively and mischievous. He delights the small group of his cousins which he bosses around. This bubbling vitality allows every hope; the mother lets herself be lulled by illusions. Unhappily, the descendant of the counts of Toulouse is marked: he carries an implacable heredity of which he will be the innocent victim.

At fourteen, Henri became a cripple, after two mild falls which were too much for his frail legs.

This is how Count Alphonse tells about both accidents:

« In May 1878, when the whole family was present in the drawing-room of the Hotel du Bosc, in Albi, when ironically the family doctor had been called for an ailing grandmother, Henri, getting up from a semi-low chair, slipped on the polished floor and broke his right leg.

« The second fracture was caused by a similarly mild fall as he was walking along with his mother, near Barèges; he rolled in the dried up bed of a torrent, no more than one or one and a half meter in depth... »

A large number of doctors and prominent professors failed to set his broken limbs satisfactorily. So it is a miserable cripple which the poor mother will drag to the well known spas: Lamalou, Barèges. But the bones will never join normally again. His shortened and thin legs will hardly uphold his large head and normal torso. To insure his limping steps, he will need the help

DOG-CART. 1880. Toulouse-Lautrec Museum, Albi.

◁ 1883, Countess A. de Toulouse-Lautrec. Toulouse-Lautrec Museum, Albi. 1887. △

CARMEN. 1885. Knoedler Gallery, New York.

The Laundress. 1888. Drawing. Museum Toulouse-Lautrec, Albi.

of a cane. Thus was the painful vision of the last descendant of the counts of Toulouse, deprived of what seemingly should have been his joy of life! However, the young cripple, worthy of his ancestors, will not let himself be disheartened.

He goes on with his studies up to the baccalaureat which he passes in Toulouse in November 1881, after having first failed in July.

He proudly announces his success to his friend Devismes:

« Swept along by the turmoil of the baccalaureat (I succeeded this time), I have neglected my friends, dictionaries and good school books. Finally the jury in Toulouse deemed me acceptable, despite the stupidity I displayed in my answers! I gave some quotations from Lucain which don't exist, and the Professor wanting to seem learned passed me with opened arms. Well, it's done... You are going to find my prose rather dull, but this is the result of the moral deflation following the examinatory tension. Let's hope for better another time. »

Here are the marks awarded to the young candidate: Latin version: tolerable; French composition: bad; Translation into English: good; construing of authors: French (Fénélon), Latin (Horace), Greek (Criton): tolerable; notions of classical literature (lyrical), of history (Louvois) of geography (the Cotention): tolerable: English (Othello): fair.

This is the full stop of Lautrec's scholarly life; he is eager to give himself entirely to his devastating passion.

* * *

Fortune was smiling upon Lautrec when he met René Princeteau.

A common liking for horses and hunting and excellent neighboring relationship sprouted a real friendship between Count Alphonse and the animal painter from Bordeaux, René Princeteau.

Although deaf, the artist was good company and his gentlemanly ways had won the aristocrat's heart. Henri received from him the advice which he needed and had not got so far, in order to improve and assert his blossoming talent. He first entered Princeteau's studio at the age of seven, and a mutual affection linked the master and his « studio nurseling. » They both showed the same affinities. In this sphere which was new to him, Lautrec was delighted to meet the real artists who were frequent visitors: Petitjean, Butin, Lindon, Loewis, Brown and Forain, whose studio was nearby.

« The boy works stoutly and is miraculously improving. he apes me like a monkey... » Princeteau wrote in his correspondence. It is true that when they went for a walk, master and pupil often sketched on the same book, some-

Gin Cocktail. 1886. Museum Toulouse-Lautrec, Albi.

times even on the same page, and only a close scrutiny can help to identify the drawings.
Princeteau persuades Henri's parents to let him follow his calling.

* * *

In March 1882, Lautrec passes the threshold of Bonnat's studio, where his southern compatriot Henri Rachou, « mass painter » from Toulouse. introduces him to his comrades who welcome Henri with unusual courtesy for this solemn occasion.

The count of Toulouse who quite naturally aroused curiosity, was spared the usual rough jokes. He quickly found himself at ease, having offered his fellow students the round of drinks required under the circumstances.

Lautrec starts working eagerly, which does not stop him, while the model rested, from parti-

Lugné-Poë in « L'Image. » 1894. Lithograph.

La Goulue. 1894. Lithograph.

cipating in the pranks indispensable for relaxation. Untiringly he applies himself as best as he can to pose his models. He would have liked to hear some encouragement from the « boss. » But very soon all he will get is: « Your colour isn't bad, but your drawing is simply terrible. »

The pupil doesn't get discouraged and redoubles his efforts. Bonnat closes his studio to give himself entirely to his increasing portrait commissions. Lautrec, together with his favorite comrades — Anquetin, Gauzi, Laval, Fauché, Emile-Bernard — decides to carry on his studies under the direction of Cormon.

He goes on scrupulously with his work and is satisfied with his new master, as expressed in a letter of February 18th, 1883 to his uncle Charles: « Cormon's corrections are much kinder than Bonnat's were. He looks at everything you show him and encourages one steadily. It might surprise you, but I don't like that so much. You see, the lashing remarks of my former master pepped me up, and I didn't spare myself. Here, I feel a little nervous and I need courage to work scrupulously at something which might satisfy Cormon too easily. For two weeks, however, he's reacted and branded a few pupils among which is myself. So I am resuming with new eagerness... »

Lautrec, however, is soon fed up with this academic discipline, and also with the models « so unlively, frozen in given attitudes, under the dull light of the sky-light. » He is attracted by the play movements and colours. He showed it in the lively drawing of horses and people where his true graphism — a strange contrast to his studio work where nothing reveals his personality — can already be found.

Following the example of a few of his friends, he happily leaves the studio, where he will only come back in 1886 to meet Van Gogh at work.

The two painters will be on friendly terms. In 1887, Lautrec paints a pastel portrait of the Hollander. They are attracted by the same models. Van Gogh's technique influences Lautrec for some time. On the other hand Henri persuades his friend to escape to the South where the light, the colour and the climate would better suit his research and needs.

* * *

Henri is now twenty years old and intends leading his artist's life as he wishes: he wants to settle down alone in a studio of his choice. His family resists. He leaves his father's house and finds shelter with his painter friends, Rachou and Grenier. He works at their place. Also, old Forest — a man of small independent means who loves artists — places a small wild garden with a few beautiful trees at his disposal, together with a small house. For a long time this remains the artist's out-of-doors studio where a number of his models sit for him: Berthe the Deaf, Gabrielle the Dancer, Justine Dieulh and many others.

In this out-of-doors studio, he also paints portraits of his friends, *Henri and Désiré Dihau*, the latter — a bassoonist at the Opéra — reading his paper (1892). *Mademoiselle Dihau at the Piano* (1892) poses in her own home. Between sittings he silently admires the portrait of his model, already painted by Degas.

However, Henri's parents, feeling the decision of their son to be irrevocable, somehow soften. They grant him large credits which enable him to live in Montmartre, the place of his choice.

He sets his studio in rue Toularque, and shares an apartment with Doctor Bourges (at 19, and then 21 rue Fontaine) a true and affectionate friend who upon the request of the Countess

The Englishman at the Moulin Rouge. 1892. Lithograph.

Yoked in Tandem. 1897. Lithograph.

looks after the young painter like a brother, Henri's taste for strong liquor is already becoming alarming.

They live together until 1893 when the Doctor gets married. Henri resents this; he feels more or less abandoned. However, he still has a faithful and serious mentor, his first cousin, Gabriel Tapié de Céleyran, who came to Paris in 1891 to study medicine. He follows Henri everywhere. The painter can't stand loneliness. but refuses to congregate with companions other than of his own choice.

Lautrec leaves the rue Tourlaque in 1897, forgetting to move a great number of canvases to his new studio at 15 rue Frochot: « It doesn't matter... » he said.

* * *

Around 1884, Lautrec could not help but know Aristide Bruant, who welcomed in his cabaret « le Mirliton » (opened in 1885 at Boulevard Rochechouart) a chosen clentele: artists, literary people and even princes !

THE LAUNDRESS. 1889. COLLECTION MRS. DORTU. DE VÉSINET. FRANCE. ▷

THE BALL AT THE MOULIN DE LA GALETTE. 1889. THE ART INSTITUTE OF CHICAGO.

DANCE AT THE MOULIN ROUGE. 1890. COLLECTION HENRY P. McILHENNY, PHILADELPHIA.

◁ THE DANCER: GABRIELLE.
1890. Toulouse-Lautrec Museum, Albi

MR. FOURCADE. 1889. Sao Paulo Museum.

HEAD OF THE GOULUE. 1891. Private Collection, Paris.

THE GOULUE AT THE MOULIN ROUGE. 1891. Private Collection.

Mr. G. H. Manuel.
1891.
Coll. Emil G. Bührle,
Zürich.

With the originality of his attire and his popular songs, Bruant was bound to attract Lautrec. A deep friendship soon developed between these two artists whose origins were so different. It lasts until 1888 when Lautrec's refined education no longer is able to withstand Bruant's triviality. Nevertheless, the singer obviously influenced the painter by introducing him through his songs to the world.

At Saint-Lazare, At the Bastille, At Montrouge, At Grenelle... These titles of Bruant's songs are also the titles of Lautrec's drawings during this period. Some of them were published in Bruant's paper « Le Mirliton, » sold for two cents at the cabaret. This is the beginning of Lautrec's spasmodic and friendly collaboration to illustrated papers, for it was useless asking him for anything at a fixed date or under compulsion.

His first drawing, *Gin Cocktail,* was published on September 26th, 1886 in the *Courrier Français.* Then *Paris Illustré, Le Rire, Figaro Illustré, La Revue Blanche, La Plume,* counted Lautrec among their contributors.

* * *

Lautrec was sixteen years old when he first illustrated a book. His young friend, Etienne Devisme, whom he met in Barèges, had asked him to draw in the text of his manuscript, the characters moving around the old mare, *Cocotte,* the mount of a country priest, which after many trials ends up her career in the Army. This humoristic tale raised the artist's enthusiasm and he made a series of zestful and humorous pen and ink drawings which already give an inkling of his genius.

In turn, his literary friends ask him to illustrate their writings:

Two volumes of the series « The Social Menagerie » by Victor Joze were edited with a lithographed cover by Lautrec. They were announced by two posters, one bearing the title of the book *Reine de Joie* and the other *Babylone d'Allemagne.* These were counted among the most daring of the master.

Lautrec signed the cover of a third book by Victor Joze, *La Tribu d'Isodore,* a novel on Jewish customs and habits; of a book by Victor Barrucand, *The Terra Cotta Chariot;* of *Ninon de Lenlcos' Example* by Jean de Tinant; of *Toys from Paris* by Paul Leclercq, and of a new edition of *Disasters of War* by Goya.

Jules Renard's *Natural Histories* bore several of Lautrec's lithographs, and Georges Clémenceau's deluxe volume *At the Foot of the Sinai* include numerous engravingsby Lautrec.

Miss Ida Heath, English Dancer, 1896. Lithograph.

Bruant had allowed Henri to hang a few of his canvases in his cabaret, thus arousing the painter's desire to reach a larger public. He took part in the exhibition of the group of XX which he followed to Brussels under the title of « free aesthetic. » As early as 1889, the *Bal at the Moulin de la Galette*, *Portrait of Mr. Fourcade* and *Study of a Woman*, which he showed at the Independants, were highly spoken of by the critics. His canvases at the Liberal Arts are noticed.

In 1892 he participates in the Impressionist and Symbolist exhibition at Le Barc de Bouteville's, rue Pelletier; the next year he shares the walls of Boussod, Valadon & Co in Montmartre with his friend Charles Maurin.

In 1900 at the Universal Exhibition, he is a member of the jury for a poster award at the Centennial and Decennial of lithography, where his works are shown. That same year he presents his most recent productions in his studio, rue Frochot. And finally at the Modern Art Salon in Bordeaux, in December, his works are shown for the last time.

* * *

Montmartre remains a vast unexplored field as far as he is concerned. From Place Pigalle to Place Clichy and up to the end of rue Tholozé at the Moulin de la Galette, balls, « café-concerts » and open bars at every step, are both pleasure and working places for Lautrec.

« His figure, always at the same place to have the same angle of vision, was becoming a legend » says Joyant. It was all the more noticeable as it offered a complete contrast with his tall cousin « the Doctor. »

« For Lautrec, » writes Mac Orlan « the ' Moulin Rouge ' was a starting point. It was, to use an expression which has become familiar since the war, a sort of regulating station where the painter attentive, holding his cane, his nose over his glass, let the pictures come to him so he could give them quality and that sort of intimate movement which was his own. »

It is indeed the Moulin Rouge which inspired Lautrec with some of his best works. In all these pages, one can find the artists who started to become known by performing in the famous music-hall whose renown they assured at the same time.

Lautrec would drink and sketch for whole nights; what might have been considered as an entertainment represented an enormous amount of work, an incessant tension from his relentless genius for observation. The documents which he gathered under the gas lamps were developed during the day time in the quiet of his studio.

Zidler, the clever manager of the Moulin Rouge, ordered in 1891 from this regular client a poster expressing the frenzy of dancing. This large poster spread all over Paris made Lautrec's name known throughout the town.

This first attempt was a triumph and marks the beginning of the painter in the art of lithography which Bonnard and his friends of the *Revue Blanche* had advised him to practice. Through this new means of expression, of which he immediately assimilated the technique, and for which he conceived a passion, Lautrec produced until his death some five hundred engravings in black, in colour and in posters of which he continously renewed the style, asserting his mastership.

He asserted this mastership immediately by the bold composition of the poster of the *Moulin Rouge* (1891) which replaced the one by Chéret. It displayed in remarkable fashion those animators of the naturalist quadrille, La Goulue and Valentin-le-Désossé. The enormous silhouette of the

The Horsewoman and the Dog. 1899. Lithograph.

dancer, placed « as screen » was a genial idea which was several years ahead of the use of « close-ups » in films.

Lautrec was following these two inseparable partners since their debuts at the *Moulin de la Galette;* he expressed in his canvas of 1889 the atmosphere of that famous music-hall.

A number of paintings and engravings show the two dancers either on the stage or mixing with the public. The latter, as a matter of fact, interested the painter as much as the artists. A « fellow-drinker » of Lautrec's, Mr. Warrener, was the subject for a beautiful coloured engraving « *The Englishman at the Moulin Rouge* » (1892) prepared from a painted study (Albi Museum). The painting *At the Moulin Rouge* (1891) is a lively page of portraits. The regular clients of the Moulin and some of the painter's friends are gathered in their familiar surroundings. Lautrec himself is there with his cousin Tapié.

La Goulue remembers Lautrec when, a fallen dancer, she asks him to paint the *Backcloth of the Booth* which she was setting up at the Place du Trone fair (1895) and which is now in the Louvre Museum.

At the *Jardin de Paris*, Lautrec will meet again with Jane Avril who was for a time one of La Goulue's partners at the Moulin for the famous quadrille; her delicate nature and natural distinction was particularly in opposition with the manners of the former washerwoman from Alsace. Lautrec had been fascinated by her demure manner which, in the street, made her « look like a school teacher. »

This is the aspect which he shows in, *Jane Avril* coming out of the Moulin Rouge 1892 and *Jane Avril with Gloves* (1892).

As for the dancer Jane Avril, who had been nick-named « The Melinite » for her spirit and dynamism, we will see her in the painting called *Jane Avril Dancing* (1892) (Louvre Museum). The painter eloquently expressed « the inspired leg which stops being a sign and becomes a writing » (Francis Jourdain).

The star is again to be seen on the coloured cover of *The Original Engraving* (1892) where the large collar of her wide cloak accentuates her emaciated face.

« The inspired leg » inspires Lautrec again for the poster Jane Avril (1893) announcing the dancer's debuts at the *Divan Japonais*. This composition is clearly under Japanese influence, as is the one of the *Jardin de Paris* (1892) where « The Melinite, » part of the public this time and sheathed in a black dress next to the critic Edouard Desjardins, listens to a boldly faceless singer with long gloved arms: Yvette Guilbert.

Among all his models, Yvette Guilbert is the one Lautrec pursued the most furiously on all the stages where the famous reciter appeared. It is also the person whose character he most violently delineated, sometimes, exaggerating her into bitter caricature. She never was satisfied with her painter whom she called « little monster, » and considered his drawing « horrible. »

The sketch for a poster (1894 Albi Museum) which Lautrec submitted to her never met with her approval, and it was only after hesitating for a long time that the entertainer agreed to sign the lithographs of two albums; their beauty totally escaped her. Thanks to Lautrec, Yvette is still vividly alive for us.

From 1892 on, the painter did not come as regularly to the shows in Montmartre.

His desire for changes, his sensuality, and his everlasting need to know and express life under all its shapes, took him elsewhere. When the lights go out in Montmartre, he went into brothels, where he was sure to find a gentle welcome, and more and more fascinating models.

His thoroughbred distinction, despite his physical deformity, his happy temperament, assures this unexpected client of the inmates' sympathy. He becomes their friend, and often their confident.

So as to know them better, he lives with them in the houses of rue Joubert, rue des Moulins, rue d'Amboise. So as not to interrupt his work, he even takes his meals there.

« Madame, » who appreciates his talent asks him to paint sixteen of her girls in medaillons, in the luxurious new parlor of the rue des Moulins of which she is very proud.

Numerous drawings, sketches and paintings date from this fruitful period between 1892 and 1894. They show the girls in their every day life: *At the Refectory, Making their Beds*, resting on a sofa, or going out for the required health inspection...

In the Parlor (Albi Museum), « a painting as pure, as unquestionable as a dish of green apples by Cézanne » (Mac Orlan), can be considered as the summing up of Lautrec's studies in this special circle.

At the « Renaissance, » Sarah Bernhardt in Phedre. 1893. Lithograph.

Lautrec widens his field of research. His love for horses, inherited from his ancestors, takes him to the race tracks. He befriends the best jockeys, admires their performances, knows the name and pedigree of the purest thoroughbreds, judges their form like an expert and calculates their odds.

It is therefore not surprising that a great number of his lithographs have been inspired by the race track world.

The Jockey, a piece of work which has become very difficult to find, is one of his best coloured engravings.

Around 1895, Tristan Bernard, manager of the Buffalo bicycle-racing-track, introduced his friend to the cycling world. Lautrec immediately adapts himself to this new circle. He speaks their idiom, befriends the champions and their trainers, follows and picks up their movements in sketches which he translates onto stone.

Tristan Bernard's portrait, in sports array, standing on the track in front of the stands, is from this period. His friend, more a literary man than a sportsman often suggested to Lautrec the captions for his drawings.

Lautrec also signed the poster « Mickael Cycles » which Spoke had asked him to do in order to promote the Simpson chain, a strange invention, which met with no success whatsoever.

Tired of being out of doors, our painter mixes up with a more bourgeois, more refined circle which he meets in different popular theatres, at the Comédie-Française and at the Opera.

Numerous lithographs which could illustrate « symbolic theatre, » and a series of portraits of well-known actors, mostly friends of Lautrec, date from this prolific period.

Here is Lugné-Poë, on the stage of the Theatre de l'Oeuvre in « The Image »; here is Sarah Bernhardt as Phèdre at the theatre Renaissance, etc...

At the Variétés theatre, Lautrec discovers Brasseur, Baron, and the graceful Marcelle Lender, who in the musical comedy « Chilperic » asserted her talent as an actress as well as her full knowledge of choreography. The painter would wait every evening, sitting in the same chair, until his model danced the bolero, and he would sketch the most characteristic movements of the dance. He completed the synthesis in the picture *Chilperic*.

Marcelle Lender's dresses, always in the best of taste would fascinate Lautrec, and the painter incited his friends to go and see her « imperial » shoulders and her « royal » back. Numerous drawings representing the actress were turned into a large series of lithographs.

At the Vaudeville, it is Réjane in « Madame San-Gêne »; at the Comédie-Française, Moreno, Bartet, Leloir, Mounet-Sully in « Antigone »; Lucien Guitry, Jane Granier; at the Théatre Libre, Gémier, Antoine, Yahne, etc...

Lautrec found some more unexpected models. He finds them at the Palais de Justice during the Panama and Lebaudy lawsuits wihch excited general interest. His curiosity finally brings him to the Hospital Saint-Louis, and into Doctor Péan's operating room, the doors of which were opened to him through his cousin Gabriel who was a student at the famous surgeon's hospital.

* * *

After an exhausting Parisian life of work and pleasure, Southern-born Lautrec needs to escape every year to the land of his fathers to breathe the family atmosphere. There, as everywhere, he

ARISTIDE BRUANT IN HIS CABARET. POSTER. 1895. ▷

MAY BELFORT. 1895. LITHOGRAPH.

LE DIVAN JAPONAIS. 1892. LITHOGRAPH. ▷

Divan Japonais
75 rue des Martyrs
Ed Fournier
directeur
Hautrec

In Bed. 1892. The Louvre Museum.

indulged in his dominant artistic passions, and, under his parents' supervision he slowed down in his need for strong drink.

He finds models around him, on the family's estate: parents, friends, servants. He is interested in agricultural life, of which he draws a few scenes: grape-gathering at Céleyran or at Malromé, an estate bought by his mother in 1883. In the drawing-room of the Chateau, Henri paints several portraits. The most touching represents his mother, the countess having her breakfast (1883); he also paints his cousin, in *Madame Pascal at the Piano*. These two pictures painted during different periods, bring forth remarkable portrait-painting qualities.

Henri is not much inspired by landscapes. Nevertheless he expresses his feeling in pictures of river banks, vines and a path in the Chateau de Céleyran garden, an amazing piece for an eighteen-year-old artist.

But he told Joyant: « The figure alone exists; landscape, is and can only be, an accessory; it can only be used to bring forward the figure's nature and character. »

It is therefore not surprising that Lautrec brought back nothing but portraits from his visits with friends in the country; at Claudon's and Grenier's in Villeneuve-sur-Morin; at Anquetin's in Etrepagny where he decorated the wall of Ancelin's inn with dance scenes.

Breakfast, (Elles). 1896. Lithograph.

In Villeneuve-sur-Yonne, at his friends the Natansons, he finds a peaceful and loving harbour. The hostess, beautiful Missia, pleasantly accepts the painter's fantasies, and he paints several portraits of this model of whom he is very fond. Missia has a good influence on him and moderates his dangerous habits. The poster (1895), for the *Revue Blanche* which Natanson manages, depicts the charming Missia playing the piano. In the artistic circle, Lautrec meets Vuillard, also a frequent guest of the house, and its best portrait painter.

* * *

Arcachon and Taussat are Henri's favorite summer resorts; he had come there as a child. He likes to be by the docks where his boat is moored; he is interested in sailing, fishing, hunting; he tames some cormorants. Precursor of nudism, Lautrec lives there as a naturist, as shown by many photographs.

* * *

The foreign countries he visited do not seem to have fascinated the painter. From his trip to Holland, which he wanted to roam with his friend Maxime Dethomas and where small boys mistook them for circus artists, the painter remembers only the pleasure he took in admiring Frans Hals in Haarlem.

In Brussels, as a guest for lunch at Van der Velde's, a pioneer of « modern style, » he is horrified by the qaudy colours on the walls of this Belgian home. He is indifferent to everything except the paintings: Breughel, Cranach, Van Eyck, Memling, Jordaens.

By accident he went to Spain. He is in the habit of following an unusual itinerary in going to Arcachon; he goes to Le Havre, and visits the « stars » — low class English concert halls on the port — while awaiting a boat for Bordeaux. In 1896, it is a ship sailing to Africa, the « Chili, » which is to take him to Bordeaux with his friend Guilbert. On the deck of that ship the painter notices a woman in a deck chair. She is beautiful and he wants to sketch her. The ship docks at Bordeaux too soon for Lautrec's taste and he decides not to leave the boat but to continue the trip with the beautiful passenger of cabin 54. But Guilbert is adamant. Lautrec finally agrees to leave the boat at Lisbon, provided the captain will cable from Dakar under Lautrec's name to the painter's Paris friends whom he wants to impress.

The Passenger of Cabin 54 has become a lithograph; it was used in a poster to announce the *Salon des Cents* (1897).

From Lisbon, our travellers go to Spain. The country disappoints Lautrec; its pleasure spots only disgust him. In Madrid and Toledo, he stops at length in the museums, enthusiastic about Greco, Velasquez and Goya.

London seems to attract him more and he stays there on several instances. He is an Anglophile from his youth, speaks the language perfectly, and feels more at ease there. However, its pleasure spots, quite different from the ones he is accustomed to in Paris, bore him.

His taste for drinking lessens, although he is offered new original cocktails in the most famous bars. He just takes the recipes for the pleasure of his Parisian friends.

In 1898, Lautrec is thirty-three. His artistic output is enormous. But his health is seriously affected. The excesses he committed with the same passion he had for drawing or painting have changed the admirable artist into a miserable weakling.

His mind is still clear; but he painfully drags his heavy silhouette around the district where he lives, never going beyond it. He becomes short tempered.

One morning, in February 1898, a serious crisis of delirium tremens necessitates Lautrec's transfer to a rest-house, the « Madrid, » in Neuilly, headed by Doctor Semelaigne. After a desintoxication cure and a few days diet the patient feels much better. He humorously describes this XVIIIth century « folly » built for happiness; later on he calls it a jail.

In a letter addressed to Maurice Joyant, Lautrec invites his friend to come and admire the garden and its beautiful trees which shades groups by the sculptor Pajou. Joyant finds the artist endeavouring to draw in a steady and mischievous hand with a woodcock feather he had found on the manure pile of the vegetable garden. The patient asks for all his material, including a lithographic stone. Lautrec still has something to say; his genius is driving him. Despite his physical misery he will go on with feverish spirits.

His friends are both surprised and happy to find the painter in the midst of creative activity, and driven more than ever by « le démon de l'art. »

At the same time his health is improving. He can walk about in the park, and is soon allowed

Woman Dressing. 1896. Lithograph.

Brandès and Leloir in « Cabotins. » 1894. Lithograph.

MONSIEUR AND MADAME AND THE DOG. 1893. MUSEUM TOULOUSE-LAUTREC, ALBI.

Justine Dieuhl. 1891.
The Louvre Museum. Formerly Collection of Prince Matsukata, Kobé, Japan.

Jane Avril. 1893. Lithograph. ▷

The Laundryman « de la Maison. » 1894. Museum Toulouse-Lautrec, Albi.

AFTER THE BATH. 1893.
PRIVATE COLLECTION, PARIS - NEW YORK.

THE BALLET OF PAPA CHRYSANTHÈME. 1892. MUSEUM TOULOUSE-LAUTREC, ALBI.

THE CLOWN, MISS CHA-U-KAO. 1895. THE LOUVRE MUSEUM.

Jane Avril

to go out with a warder whose portrait he paints — *My Keeper* (Albi Museum). He stays strictly sober, as prescribed, but gets the « keeper » very drunk. He brings in a hollow cane carefully prepared for this illicit use his own little share of alcohol.

As soon as he was admitted to the rest-house of Neuilly, ignorant and malicious journalists spread the most inaccurate rumors about the reasons for Lautrec's confinement. In the Journal one could read: « ... Lautrec's vocation was to go to a rest-house. He was committed yesterday and it will now be insanity which will openly sign these pictures, drawings and posters where until now, it was anonymous. » In the *Echo de Paris*: « We are wrong to pity Lautrec, we should envy him... the only place where happiness can be found is indeed in a padded cell in a mad-house... »

To these nasty and false articles, Arsène Alexandre answers violently in the *Figaro*: « A few days ago everybody buried the painter Toulouse-Lautrec, a basically Parisian figure, and there has not been one Parisian who took pains to find out whether he was still alive before giving him a funeral speech... A legend is born among the public and in the small circles, and nobody took the trouble to check it. What has been written about Lautrec is stupefying. »

While different and contradictory opinions about Lautrec's behavior were being offered, the painter surprised and pleased his friends by drawing from memory and with an extraordinary accuracy, his outstanding series, *At the Circus*. He expressed with absolute lucidity these scenes which he had watched so often and at such length. He there achieved an exceptional mastership, especially with such simple means. These drawings can take their place next to Goya's *Caprices* which, according to André Lhote, they equal. They are the epitome of Lautrec's art.

This production of some fifty pieces enables the doctors of the « Madrid to sign the release of their famous patient on May 20th 1898. « I bought my freedom with my drawings » said Lautrec. This makes him feel like travelling. From now on his companion will be Viaud, a friend of the family, who has been requested to look after him.

The painter and his mentor leave for Arcachon, and following the custom go to Le Havre to take a ship for Bordeaux. Before getting on board the ship, Lautrec, as was his habit, goes to visit the « stars. » A blond barmaid fascinates him so much that he wants her as a model. As soon as he has received his painting gear for which he had cabled to Maurice Joyant, Lautrec skeches in red chalk the profile of the pretty Miss Dolly, and paints her portrait. These two pieces (Albi Museum) are among his best. He sends them to Joyant with the following rather witty note: « A painting with a new, larger treatment, in the manner of the best Grecos! »

Lautrec and Viaud finally leave for Bordeaux and Taussat where they take a cure of « air, sun and sea. »

By the end of 1899, Lautrec goes back to Paris and resumes his Montmartre life. He is eager to see his friends again and sends them the following invitation: « Mr. Henri de Toulouse-Lautrec would be most flattered if you would accept a cup of milk, Saturday, May 15th, in his studio, 5 (15) rue Frochot. »

In November he visits the Universal Exhibition where nothing seems to interest him except Japan, the Javanese dancers, and Cleo de Mérode who is the subject of some of his drawings.

Once more he returns to Crotoy, to Le Havre, to Honfleur. But this time when he faithfully goes to Le Havre to embark, he is greatly disappointed; the « stars » have been closed down. After having spent the fall in Arcachon he stays in Bordeaux where he works frenetically.

He paints portraits of the violinist Dancla, and of Paul Viaud dressed as a British admiral which later hangs in the dining-room of the Chateau de Malromé. He paints race track pictures

Miss Marcelle Lender. 1895. Lithograph.

The Milliner, Renée Vert. 1893. Lithograph.

Leloir and Moreno in « Les Femmes Savantes. » 1894.

NAPOLÉON. 1895. LITHOGRAPH. ▷

THE RECEPTION ROOM OF THE «RUE DES MOULINS.» 1894.
MUSEUM TOULOUSE-LAUTREC, ALBI.

RESTING. 1896. PRIVATE COLLECTION. ▷

ALFRED LA GUIGNE. 1894.
NATIONAL GALLERY OF ART, WASHINGTON D. C. COLLECTION CHESTER DALE.

◁ MISS BÉATRICE TAPIÉ DE CÉLEYRAN. 1896. COLLECTION ITTLESON, NEW YORK.

◁ Femme de Maison. 1894. Museum Toulouse-Lautrec, Albi.

THE GOULUE DANCING. 1895.
DÉTAIL: L'ALMÉE. THE LOUVRE MUSEUM.

◁ LA TOILETTE. 1896. THE LOUVRE MUSEUM.

The Clown, Miss Cha-U-Kao. 1896. Collection Oscar Reinhart, Winterthur, Switzerland.

IN THE LOGE. 1897. COLLECTION METTLER, ST. GALL, SWITZERLAND.

Miss May Belfort.
1895.
Collection Bernheim
Jeune, Paris.

and makes many drawings. Concerning the theatre, he immortalized the truculent star of the *Belle Hélène*, « Cocyte, » in a watercolour drawing.

He is enthusiastic about the lusty atmosphere of the Opera « Messaline » staged for the first time in Bordeaux. Actors and participants will live again in drawings, lithographs and paintings.

Lautrec leaves Bordeaux and comes to Paris where he arrives around the end of April 1901, feeling very weak. However, his friends are surprised by his eagerness to work. He classifies or finishes paintings which he had dropped, initials or signs the pieces which he considers as being his best achievements. He paints the portraits of Coolus, Rivière, Raquin, Joyant... women washing up or dressing, nudes, and horsemen and horsewomen which he sketches at the Bois where he goes daily. He is still attracted by the stone, but the poster *La Gitane* (The Gipsy) will be the last of this sort of production. A few engravings will be made just before he leaves Paris forever in July 1901.

He knows, and his friends know, that this separation is final. Lautrec will fight, however...

He settles down at Tausset, hoping that the sea air will help him. On the contrary, his state quickly worsens; he is paralysed.

The Countess, who rushed to the side of her dear child, has him taken to Malromé. He seems happy to find there the memories of a dear past, surrounded by his mother's tender love, in the family house. During these last days, he paints a piece in a new manner — *Examination at the Medical Faculty* — where he pictured his cousin Gabriel Tapié de Céleyran upholding his thesis.

Alas, Lautrec is getting weaker by the day and the end is nearing. Count Alphonse has come to the bedside of his dying son, « not in the least embarrassed to find himself under the same roof as his wife whom he had long since deserted » (Mary Tapié).

The last affectionate words of the dying painter were addressed to his mother, his only love: « Maman... you... only you! »

Pascal and Gabriel Tapié, his cousins, assist him as he receives the last sacraments. Also was present, Adeline, the faithful chambermaid who had brought up Henri and whom he had often caricaturized as a mouse.

Henri de Toulouse-Lautrec-Monfa died at the age of thirty-seven on the morning of September 9th. He was first buried at Saint-André-du-Bois but the Countess had his body transferred to Verdelais when plans to displace the cemetery made her fear that her son's repose might be disturbed.

* * *

Following the death of his son, Count Alphonse expressed his grief to his friend René Princeteau:

« Malromé, September 18, 1901, 3:30 evening.

« My dear friend, I am going to hurt you deeply. Your protégé of the old days when you were staying at Perey's, your protégé who had made such good use of the example you were affectionately setting for him under the lamp of the old « pension » which we miss, for we were all young then and full of hope and reality has been very hard·and full of disappointments for all of us... Henri, my son, « the kid, » as you used to call him, died tonight at two fifteen. I had arrived four or five hours earlier and saw the horrible, unforgettable sight of this boy, the best of all hearts, on which were weeping in advance those who, like yourself, had found out the trea-

Chocolat, Dancing. 1896. Drawing. Museum Toulouse-Lautrec, Albi.

At the Moulin Rouge. Entrance of Cha-U-Kao. 1896. Museum Toulouse-Lautrec, Albi.

Back-stage of the Folies-Bergères. 1896. Drawing. Museum Toulouse-Lautrec, Albi.

At the Circus. The Animal Trainer. 1899. Lithograph.

sures of his loyalty and friendship, once one knew him. His wide opened eyes did not see anything anymore after three or four days of delirium. He was good and gentle, hardly recriminating against anything or anybody, he who had suffered so much from his appearance which caused people to turn around and stare, generally with more pity than mockery.

« He no longer suffers. Let us hope for another life where we can meet again with no obstacles to eternal sympathy. »

« ... I cannot cease to weep for my poor and harmless Henri who was never unkind to his father. A lamb of God, so gay, despite the horrible sufferings of his childhood. Dear child, in God we will meet forever, where there will no doubt be no more heirarchical constraint between a father and his descendants, whether wanted or not, and resulting from the furious attraction of true lovers, and not from unmarriageable people of the same condition. »

After reading these pitiful lines, it is hard to believe that Lautrec's father was so often charged with indifference. One would be justified in thinking he had belated regrets, regrets which can also be applied to the dreadful consequences of intermarriage.

One knows that Henri's two accidents coincided with the stop of his growth and that his lower limbs never became strong again. This is an abnormal case in a fourteen-year-old adolescent, and it remains a problem because of the lack of a precise diagnosis from the medical authorities of that time.

More than half a century after his death, doctors have tried to determine the causes of this frailness of bone which changed the painter into a dwarf.

In a thesis which he recently upheld in the Medical Faculty of Montpellier, Pierre Devoisins, a young doctor from Albi, puts forward an hypothesis which seems to bring the expected explanations. He studied everything, the painter's psychology, his sexual attitude, his taints, his passion for strong drink. He comments: « Enslaved to his exacerbated sensibility and sensuality, Lautrec's nature drove him to an uncurbed pursuit of subtle or excessive emotions. » Also, as has been written elsewhere: « Lautrec pursued love in a reckless fashion without rhyme or reason. » This explains that he did not escape catching syphilis. Thanks to his alcoholism, the general paralysis which affected him shortly before he died did not have time to strike to the last stage — complete and total decay.

In any case the one and the other united their efforts to bring about a premature death.

Some critics, have tried to explain, by using psychoanalysis, that Lautrec's love for certain circles and the salient feature of his talent — « composed of bitter perversity and of dreadful bliss, » one of them wrote — was caused by his being a cripple.

René Huyghe, in a study published in « L'Amour de l'Art » (1931) answers to this « Pagliacci's literature »: « His infirmity does not bring him a systematic pessimism eager for depravity; it led him to live in a circle of unconventionality and festivity where his silhouette was no more than an unintentional eccentricity among many other intentional ones, and where it gave him a sort of popularity instead of making him ridiculous as it did everywhere else. He escaped into this sort of life, as he escaped into drinking. All he did, was to use, with no evil intention, his ruthless talent for observing, which he would have used in any other circle where he might have lived. If he accentuated its ugliness it is because his temperament induced him to underline ' characteristics ' and because the world in which he lived could not show him anything else. »

Do not the drawings Lautrec made when a boy, before the accidents which crippled him, bring forth the same desire to accentuate the nature of his models? And didn't Lautrec make innumerable burlesque and unflattered self-portraits?

Profile of a Woman. 1899. Drawing.
Museum Toulouse-Lautrec, Albi.

The Englishwoman of « The Star » at Havre. 1899. Drawing. Museum Toulouse-Lautrec, Albi.

THE ENGLISH GIRL OF THE « STAR » IN HAVRE. 1899. MUSEUM TOULOUSE-LAUTREC, ALBI.

BERTHE BADY. 1897.
MUSEUM TOULOUSE-LAUTREC, ALBI.

THE MILLINER. 1900. MUSEUM TOULOUSE-LAUTREC, ALBI.

MESSALINE. 1900. COLLECTION EMIL G. BÜHRLE, ZURICH.

Cocyte in « La Belle Hélène. » Bordeaux. 1900. Watercolour. Museum Toulouse-Lautrec, Albi.

Eros Crippled. 1894. Lithograph

Cecy Loftus. 1895. Lithograph.

No doubt, he suffered from the physical disability which prevented him from taking part in the brilliant society life to which his birth entitled him, and forced him to abandon his favorite sports.

Of course, he always showed everybody a mask of gaity and festivity. But disappointment is expressed in the confession he made to his friend Alfred Edwards: « One paints for lack of anything better. » It is, however, impossible to think that fatality alone was responsible for Lautrec's calling. If at first he considered art as an exhilarating distraction in which he found a refuge, his eager passion which started when he was still a child already told of his predestination. Therefore one can truly assume that had Lautrec been a normal man, he would not have been able to resist the inner flame that was consuming him and which would have overtaken whatever resistance his family might have opposed to his choice of a career.

* * *

It is not surprising that Lautrec's art, although so close to tradition and classicism, was not welcomed by his contemporaries. The « officials » rejected him; the public did not understand him any better. His taste, distorted by the formulas of an anecdotical academism, prevented him from getting close to the great masters, the new painters, or from having any artistic affiliation with them. The Impressionists, and before them Millet, Daubigny, Corot, had known the same ostracism. When Lautrec died, one could read in the *Echo de Paris*:

« The caricaturist H. de Toulouse-Lautrec has just died in a rest-house, after frantic crisis, after an emphatic and dreadful struggle towards recovery and towards life... Three years ago he had already been committed, but had been able to get out of the horrible mad-house... Among the painters of his time, he will leave the mark of his curious and evil talent; the talent of a distorted human being who sees everything around him ugly, and exaggerates life's ugliness. »

Le Courrier Français, le Temps and some other newspapers took up, in the same tone, the same kind of malevolent criticism.

However, a few more experienced critics were capable of defining and appreciating the true value of Lautrec's art: Octave Mirbeau, Gustave Geoffroy, Roger-Marx, and Huc the editor of *La Dépêche de Toulouse*. Arsène Alexandre, in particular, stood up for his friend, both on the artistic and on the human level.

Lautrec's impulsive nature never allowed him to bend to any conformism. He acquired and asserted his personality by letting himself be led by his temperament and his domineering tastes.

Princeteau encouraged the blossoming of his talent. The academic discipline to which he deliberately forced himself during three years in the studios of Bonnat and of Cormen made him conscious of his craft.

Lautrec's personality which already strongly emerges in his first drawings, seems smothered under the stiff rulers of his masters. But as soon as the artist is freed from their constraint, his personality comes out again and develops. It won't be altered despite the influences to which Lautrec was susceptible at the end of the XIXth century at which time his contemporaries were giving a new face to art, through revolutionary methods. Attempts and successes in this field must have attracted our painter, who loved anything new. In his rather scarce correspondence, Lautrec never mentioned what he thought of these innovations, but there there is no doubt that he was following them with enthusiasm.

Quite naturally, his first master's influence can be detected in Lautrec's first pieces, especially in those preceding his admission at Bonnat's: horses, riders, and carriages with horses, which were both master's and pupil's favorite themes.

Lautrec's stays at Bosc and at Céleyran inspired him with a few landscapes. But he preferred painting the land workers in the Aveyron or Aude country. The works painted during this period — *A Worker at Céleyran* (1882) and *Routy* (1883) — show

his attraction to painters who after Boudin, and following the example of Bastien-Lepage, were trying to put more light in their paintings by pictur ing the figure as part of the landscape.

A reflection of Berthe Morisot's sensitive and delicate chromatism can be found in the portrait of the *Countess at Breakfast* (1883), a true page of love. Looking at her sitting on a bench in the garden brings to mind the *Woman with a Sunshade* or the *Woman Sewing* which are at the Museum of Pau. On the other hand *The Countess Reading in the Drawing-room* (1887) reveals a technique which is close to that of Seurat. Memories of Whistler's dulled harmonies appear in *Woman Sitting on a Bench at Céleyran* (1885).

Désiré Dihau Reading in the Garden of Old Forest (1891) is definitely in the Impressionist manner and so are several portraits of women done under the shade of this out-of-doors studio.

Henri Dihau evokes a figure escaped from one of Raffaelli's paintings; its strokes remind one of those of the painter « of provincial people and petit bourgeois » who was also, in his days, an innovator.

The long strokes used by Lautrec in his portrait of *Hélène* (1888) do not surprise us as they are characteristic of Van Gogh's manner with whom Lautrec worked — for a short period, it is true — using the same models and exchanging ideas about art. Lautrec's pastel portrait of the Hollander (1886) shows a technique closely related to that of the doomed and anathemized painter.

Lautrec enthusiastically admired Degas. Like him he was fascinated by « humanism »; like

him, inspired by the theatre, the circus, the concert... modern life. For his part Degas appreciated the young artists's talent and complimented him thus, following one of his exhibitions: « Well there, Lautrec, one can see that you belong to the fraternity ! »

Forain's drawing, large and synthetic, was considered by Lautrec as an example of « fine drawing. » And he always admired the watercolour portrait the master had made, out of friendship, of Count Alphonse.

Following Lautrec in his trips, we learn the names of a few old masters who particularly attracted his attention: Greco, Velasquez, Rembrandt, Jordaens, Breughel...

Their influence is not directly visible in Lautrec's paintings; but he made use of their lessons for he found in their works the plastic perfection towards which he strove through new means.

In all and every field Lautrec admired « good workmanship. »

Like most great artists of the XIXth century — and especially Degas to whom Japanese art had been revealed in 1889 — Lautrec acquired from his oriental masters the audacity of bold page-setting, with expressive diagonals and a taste for rhythm and soberness which is particularly clear in his posters.

Here, in the large posters (Bruant) Lautrec's technique meets Gauguin's mural art and plastic power. It can be found again in the master's last works: *At the Races* and *Examination at the Paris Medical Faculty* (1901); some have seen in this new manner the painter's « weariness. » But shouldn't one rather consider it as a new direction of his vision which death prevented him from following?

* * *

Sketcher, painter, lithographer, Lautrec welcomed with the same enthusiasm any process which allowed him to express himself. His genius asserted itself in every manner and bestows amazing unity to his works.

Whatever the means, he always remains the ruthless, uncompromising observer who « dissects his models in a sort of moral and psychological nakedness. » (Lassaigne). None equals Lautrec in his capacity to seize the essentials of a face, of a gesture, in a final synthesis, spontaneously born from an immediate mental analysis. Thus he attains the highest peaks of art.

One would judge the painter superficially if one considered only his studies — none the less admirable — thrown down from life, in the fever of creation, and simply on unprepared cardboard.

To allow his brush to follow his thought quickly enough and to cover the absorbant surface of the cardboard, Lautrec had to use oil painting strongly deluted in petrol. His painting then took on a chalky and dull aspect which could make it be mistaken for gouache or pastel which he very seldom used. When he has painted on wood or canvas, the matter is richer due to the lack of absorption.

To tell the truth, Lautrec never tried to have a rich mixture; « skillful cooking » was not his forte. If he didn't like what he had done, instead of « correcting » by superimposing new layers, he would take off the whole paint with petrol and start afresh. This is the way he proceeded for the portrait of Maurice Joyant, the result, his patient model tells us, of seventy-two sittings.

Lautrec's painting does not show his sensual temperament, nor does it show in any of his works inspired by the lowliest world. His figures always remain what they are; they always retain a decency and a distinction which is not found in many of his contemporaries' works; the latter often bringing forth an ambiguous sensuality caused by the vulgarity of their realism.

His qualities as a painter are more apparent in the works of his early youth which show less boldness and decision. But as his line achieves its aim as means of expression, drawing becomes more important to him than colour. He draws with his brush as much as he paints. However, his always distinguished colours are delicately set; first in hachure to suggest the relief, then in large flats, when through his experience with posters, he understood the plastic power of this technique.

His harmonies with their delicate tones reveal his sensitive nature. This is especially clear in his lithographs where the qualities of the painter are enhanced by the draftman's qualities. He starts working on stone with the same ease and with as steady a hand as he had on paper, with no need of tracer or transfer to complete his drawing. His line is « naturally coloured » like that of Daumier, to use Baudelaire's expression. There is a certain link between the two masters, through their expressive and shortered graphism, attracted by the theatre's artificial lights.

Lautrec uses soft pencils voluptuously to express the infinite scale of values. In his engravings he plays with colours as arranging a delicate symphony; on posters it blares out like a brass band.

Lautrec has sometimes been classified among the Impressionists, although he never followed their scientific theories or their optics. In contact with them he lightened his palette, but he never sought — as they did — to stick the fugitive appearances of light in one theme. « Impressionist of Movement » would better qualify our painter.

Nor can he be put in the Nabi group which belongs to his generation; some of which were his friends. To which School, then, should he be linked? He himself would have answered this question with a roar of laughter, unless he had used Gauguin's sally: « To think that there are Schools! For what? To teach everyone to follow the same road as their neighbor? »

Without sharing the misgivings of the painters of his time, Lautrec followed his own road — the road to independence which was also followed by Cézanne, Van Gogh, Gauguin. He remains, apart from the currents of French painting of the XIXth century, a strongly original master.

Today Lautrec's works have become classic, understood, and unanimously admired. His works, an immense effort of only twenty-five years, bring forth an exceptional genius of whom French art is justly proud.

An Examination before the Faculty of the Paris School of Medicine.
The last picture painted by Toulouse-Lautrec. Museum Toulouse-Lautrec, Albi.

BIBLIOGRAPHY

BAZIN (Germain) - *L'Epoque impressionniste;* Tisné, Paris, 1947.

BELLET (L. Charles) - *Le Musée d'Albi;* Albi, avril 1951.

BORGESE (Leonardo) - *Toulouse-Lautrec;* Ulrico Hoepli; Milan, 1945.

COOPER (Douglas) - *Toulouse-Lautrec;* Nouvelles éditions françaises; Paris, 1955.

COQUIOT (Gustave) - *Toulouse-Lautrec;* Paris, Blaizot, 1913.

DELAROCHE-VERNET-HENRAUX (Marie) - *Toulouse-Lautrec dessinateur;* Paris « Quatre Chemins-Editart », 1949.

DELTEIL (Loys) - *Le peintre graveur illustré, tomes X et XI: Henri de Toulouse-Lautrec;* Paris, 1920.

DEVOISINS (Dr. Louis) - *Toulouse-Lautrec;* Imprimerie Coopérative du Sud-Ouest, Albi, 1956. — *Henri de Toulouse-Lautrec: Essai d'étude clinique. — Ses maladies. — Sa mort.* — Thèse présentée à la Faculté de Médecine de Montpellier 1958.

DORIVAL (Bernard) - *Les étapes de la peinture française contemporaine, tome 1 « De l'Impressionnisme au Fauvisme »* Gallimard, Paris, 1943.

DORTU (Mme M. G.) - *L'étrange Toulouse-Lautrec, dans « Art et Style »;* Robert Lang, édit. Paris, 1951.

DORTU (Mme M. G.) - *Toulouse-Lautrec;* Nouvelles Editions du Chêne, Paris, 1952.

DORTU (Mme M. G.) - GRILLAERT (Madeleine), ADHEMAR (Jean) - *Toulouse-Lautrec en Belgique;* Berggruen et Cᵒ, Paris, 1953.

FLORISOONE (Michel) - *Connaissance de Lautrec - in « Art et Style »,* Robert Lang, édit. Paris, 1951.

FOSCA (François) - *Lautrec;* Albums Druet; Libraire de France, Paris, 1928.

GAUZI (François) - *Lautrec et son temps.* David Perret, Paris, 1954.

GEORGES-MICHEL (Georges) - *De Renoir à Picasso. Les peintres que j'ai connus;* Arthème Fayard, Paris, 1954.

GUERIN (Marcel) - *Lithographies de Toulouse-Lautrec* Grund, Paris, 1948.

HANSON (L. et H.) - *La vie tragique de Toulouse-Lautrec;* Ed. Corré; Paris. 1958.

JEDLICKA (Gothard) - *Henri de Toulouse-Lautrec;* Bruno Cassirer, Berlin, 1929.

HUYGHE (René) - *Aspects de Toulouse-Lautrec dans « l'Amour de l'Art »;* avril 1931.

JOURDAIN (Francis) - *Toulouse-Lautrec;* Editions Jean Marguerat, Lausanne, 1950. *Toulouse-Lautrec;* Braun, Paris, 1951.

JOURDAIN (Francis) - ADHEMAR (Jean) - *Toulouse-Lautrec;* P. Tisné, édit. Paris, 1952.

JOYANT (Maurice) - *Henri de Toulouse-Lautrec, peintre;* Floury, édit, Paris, 1926. *Henri de Toulouse-Lautrec, dessins, estampes, affiches;* Floury, édit, Paris, 1926.

JULIEN (Edouard) - *Dessins de Toulouse-Lautrec;* Monaco, Les Documents d'Art, 1942. *Dessins de Lautrec;* Collection Plastique; Edit. Braun, 1951. *Les affiches de Toulouse-Lautrec;* Editions du Livre, André Sauret, Monte-Carlo-Paris, 1951. *Lautrec vu par ses contemporains* in « Art et Style », nᵒ 13, mai 1951.

KOCH (Schaub) - *Psychanalyse d'un peintre moderne;* l'Edition litéraire internationale, Paris, 1935.

LAPPARENT - *Les maîtres de l'art moderne: Toulouse-Lautrec;* les éditions Rieder, Paris, 1927.

LAPRADE (Jacques de) - *Lautrec.* Aimery Somogy, Paris, 1954.

LASSAIGNE (Jacques) - *Toulouse-Lautrec.* Editions Hypérion, Paris, 1939. *Toulouse-Lautrec;* Skira, édit. Genève, 1953.

LECLERCQ (Paul) - *Autour de Toulouse-Lautrec ;* H. Floury, édit. Paris, 1921.

MAC-ORLAN - *Lautrec, peintre de la lumière froide ;* H. Floury, édit. Paris, 1934.

MACK (Gerstle) - *Toulouse-Lautrec, texte anglais ;* Alfred Knopf, édit. New York, 1938.

MARTRINCHARD (Robert) - *Princeteau, professeur et ami de Toulouse-Lautrec.* Bordeaux, 1956.

MARX (Claude-Roger) - *Lithographies en couleurs de Toulouse-Lautrec.* F. Hazan, édit. Paris, 1948.
Yvette Guilbert vue par Toulouse-Lautrec ; Au pont des Arts, Paris, 1950.

MELBYE (Herbert) - *H. de Toulouse-Lautrec ;* Tilskueren, juin 1931 ; Gyldendalske Boghandel Nordisk Forlag.

NATANSON (Thaddée) - *Un Toulouse-Lautrec ;* Cailler, édit. Genève.

PERRUCHOT (Henri) - *La vie de Toulouse-Lautrec,* Hachette, Paris, 1958.

PICASSE (Jules) - *Toulouse-Lautrec.* Imprimerie Coopérative du Sud-Ouest, Albi, 1907.

ROTZLER (Willy) - *Affiches de Toulouse-Lautrec.* Ed. Holbein, Bâle. Editions du Chêne, Paris, 1946.

TAPIÉ DE CÉLEYRAN (Mary) - *Notre oncle Lautrec ;* Cailler, édit. Genève, 1953.

TOURETTE (Gilles de la) - *Lautrec ;* Trésors de la Peinture françaises. Skira, Genève, 1938.

VENTURI (Lionello) - *De Manet à Lautrec ;* Albin Michel, Paris, 1953.

VINDING (Ole) - *Toulouse-Lautrec ;* Nyt Nordisk Forlag Arnol Busk, Copenhague, 1947.

WARNOD (André) - *Les peintres de Montmartre ;* La Renaissance du Livre, Paris, 1928.

ILLUSTRATIONS